NO DEPRESSION IN HEAVEN

ALSO BY RYAN FITZPATRICK

POETRY

*Coast Mountain Foot**
Fake Math
*Fortified Castles**
Sunny Ways

EDITOR

Why Poetry Sucks:
An Anthology of Humorous Experimental Canadian Poetry
(with Jonathan Ball)

* Published by Talonbooks

NO DEPRESSION IN HEAVEN

POEMS

ryan fitzpatrick

TALONBOOKS

Talonbooks
9259 Shaughnessy Street, Vancouver, British Columbia, Canada V6P 6R4
talonbooks.com

Talonbooks is located on xʷməθkʷəy̓əm, Sḵwx̱wú7mesh, and səlilwətaɬ Lands.

First printing: 2025

Typeset in Warnock
Printed and bound in Canada on 100% post-consumer recycled paper

Cover photograph *Cowboy* by Mohammad Mirzajani via unsplash.com
Cover photograph *Clouds* by Jesus Meireles via unsplash.com

Talonbooks acknowledges the financial support of the Canada Council for the Arts, the Government of Canada through the Canada Book Fund, and the Province of British Columbia through the British Columbia Arts Council and the Book Publishing Tax Credit.

Library and Archives Canada Cataloguing in Publication

Title: No depression in heaven : poems / ryan fitzpatrick.
Names: Fitzpatrick, Ryan, 1978- author.
Identifiers: Canadiana 2025017894X | ISBN 9781772016956 (softcover)
Subjects: LCGFT: Poetry.
Classification: LCC PS8611.I893 N6 2025 | DDC C811/.6—dc23

The style I use mainly is a whole-tone slur which gives more of a lonesome cowboy sound. You hit a note and slide almost simultaneously to another.

—FLOYD CRAMER

But no one knows for certain and so it's all the same to me.

—IRIS DeMENT

TRACK LIST

SIDE A

SIDE B

PRINCE ALBERT GRAND OLE OPRY 8:30 - 9:00 PM
[October 24, 2025]

AS BROADCAST

ANNOUNCER: From the Ryman Auditorium in Nashville, Tennessee, the country music capital of the world, it's your Grand Ole Opry, presented by PRINCE ALBERT, the world's most popular smoking tobacco.

(TRAIN WHISTLE)

MUSIC: "GONNA HAVE A GOOD TIME TONIGHT". . . RYAN FITZPATRICK AND THE BOW RIVER BACHELORS

ANNOUNCER: Yes, it's the Grand Ole Opry! The same program with the same people you've been listening to for the last century. Only tonight we've left the confines of the radio dial to reach you through this book of poetry, published in Vancouver, Canada, and distributed from the great Atlantic Ocean to the wide Pacific shore. And now friends, here is George Hay, the "Solemn Ol' Judge," our master of ceremonies!

(APPLAUSE)

HAY: Thank you, thank you. And hello everybody. For the next hundred some pages, we will present nothing but realism. It will be down-to-earth for the earthy. Tonight from this stage, we city slickers will dress up in our finest rural, white rusticity, playing your favourite folk tunes from the Appalachian hills just as A.P. Carter extracted them. Thanks to the folks at the National Life and Accident Insurance Company, we are able to bring you this dangerously nostalgic cornucopia of old-time music week after week, giving you the chance to reflect on this ever-constant string of latter days, to sing along to a worried song about the precarious state of your place in the world, and to wonder what kinds of blessed assurance and INsurance you might need for the days ahead. This station's call sign WSM stands for "We Shield Millions," which is National Life's motto. But also remember their other motto: "An unsaved man is never ready to receive salvation until he is convinced he is lost without it."

(APPLAUSE)

HAY: The Grand Ole Opry house is packed and
we're ready to start the shindig! If
these ain't the good times, what is? Ryan
2 Fitzpatrick and his Bow River Bachelors
are ready to start us off with a good ol'
breakdown. Let 'er go, boys!

MUSIC: <u>"THE WHOLE-TONE SLUR OF THE LONESOME COWBOY" . . . RYAN FITZPATRICK AND THE BOW RIVER BACHELORS</u>

SIDE A

THE WHOLE-TONE SLUR OF THE LONESOME COWBOY

Somewhere
along the line
information
became as
traditional
as anything else
so fiddles down, boys
let's take a nap
and figure out how
to slip like a
fish slides
off the coast's
new inter-
continental micro-
plastic fantasia

Opposites
defend one
on another
in slow places
as curational as
low friends lowing
the class drawbridge
vibe check
to the last
last awful Amarillo
its road cued
to the sevens
roped back
from the low-
paced lope of
the high-value
scoot

And soon
they'll carry
stimulation away
wreathed in
elegy as a treat
for rodeo-ready
hearts not here
for the roiling
hillbilly spycraft
of wall-tearing
nostalgia

I heard a luke-
warm payment
in the winds of
a low-stakes carry
that hammers
this land all over
when being easy
ain't easy's
scale-side poured
ship dynamic
played over plate
hammered into
full Bugatti man-
scavation lying
poised for
the ripened
purchase moment

Cost, cost
on the range

where the dear
antihope in a place
coped by small
incremental
stat buffs like
how many
secret presidential
subbasements
back love's basic
marquee promise
to build back
the price of each
little ply

Do you take
this data to be
your bedded
blight, repro
man and his
cool, cool ought
lowing both
headlights by
and by word
by and by risk
replacement
where repace
meant knowing
when to fold
and when to fold
meant the held
hand of intimacy
threw me as dice

tossed like
plywood girded
against replacement

If my bailed swap
squares off with
pride's smashed
Okie kingmaking
the lonesome whip
wills road and trail
to rent teardrop
nexting, outscrolled
and outsung, until
the next gambler
falls, his bus ad
projecting love
for the fratty
spur sidling
grave robbed
man of earns
by no earns
sting and explode

If I took one
and replaced it
with another's
front-porch
sea-seeing
a swap that had love
one thing Daddy made
a juridical
pyramid scheme
midlining the dollar's

flat-faced anxiety
its lateral bubble
shooting Reno
just to watch
would it slotfire
its F-150 feed
until a hundred
Laredos bloom?

HOLLOW SQUARE

I'm going to fake a grip on that old gospel ship
Extract a scar across the sky
I'm gonna shit out brinks 'til Heaven sinks
As I surge this world's goodbye

I've leveraged circling to total everything
All your debts with me you'll square
I'm going to make a line that only knows to rise
'Til we're bailing out the air

I'm going to crack my whip on that new condo strip
I'm renovicting all the sky
I'm gonna cry critique 'til Heaven tweaks
Our mistakes until they're crime

It takes financing's taste to bite into the waste
Of spending's time in prayer
And when that ship inflates, I'll leave this world with haste
As our failure costs the air

This tune is not my tome, it's just amassing blue
My complaints and my copes are all beyond the true
Where ev'ry idling engine has all jawed on so bored
And I can't feel at home in this world anymore

O'er my landed glow, there is no fountain there
Its spouts don't saint Victoria while singeing everywhere
I swing the oathsome smears over the words I floor
When I can't feel at home in this world anymore

O hymn, you know, I trend no trail like you
If real estate's my home, Landlord, what should I do?
An angling stake of street in Heaven's open pour
Where I can't feel at home in this world anymore

Ever-surveying ease, that's one rope I'll throw
Across the fix with Jesus, so the growth won't slow
History passed through even though I locked the door
And I can't feel at home in this world anymore

Three thousand miles, an empired breadth
That grid-lined fetish plans
Its offsets sprawling, desperate
Must be made by human hands

It won't be long 'til value streaks
Right through White City's square
With fifty miles of elbow room
On either side to spare

When the state's clanged tide makes the other side
Framed astride the recency
There'll be scarce room spared as we enter there
There'll be room to make more room for me

For the fates are plied if they're called offside
To discard my lowering boom
In the white hand of what's left and
Fifty miles of elbow room

Come trad glory when profit is over
I'll fly away
To my family's hot palatial shore
I'll fly away

I'll fly away, O Boeing
I'll fly away
E'er I link, Hallelujah, fix to fix
I'll fly away

Just a few more bleary deals and then
I'll fly away
To the stars where History can't reach
I'll fly away

I'll fly away, O Glory
I'll fly away, past the mourning
Up a line, Hallelujah, buy and buy
I'll fly away

DEFACEMENT SWEET

And then everyone and I
stopped breathing, over and over
lungs cranked through the endless
doomscroll of the universe

And somewhere along the way
complexity became informational
and I learned how tough
it is to lean on anyone

I never expected to lean so much
from the churn listening me
deep in a vast private correction
that mines people as sourcepoint

I never realized that it's better
to siphon out my social life
to set my sense of loneliness
on fire, but just the sense of it

Isn't life a randomizer of itself
linked to the trending comforts
of a technological bubble, heating
up water with the power of song?

Isn't the clobbering artifice of
the county fair too real to be
moulded regression chum spread
across too much Texas toast?

And I would lasso you the moon
but why would you want it
when it's too big to fit
in your tiny garden suite?

I know love is a product of its time
but what is the timing of its
branding campaign, broadened by
a Bud Light patenting trampoline

I love you and your marketing
strategy's funding needs, defenced
from the white-inked abstraction
of a power-washed rental property

I love the simple tale of the
chemtrail's redline across the cork
as it peels the neighbourhood
right down to its cell reception

A touch of moonlight in my
development permit turns your
gaslighting ornament to trip
over a moistened-eye application

If I look for love in all the right
replacements, maybe I'll find
my face sweetly decomposed
by a small-lunged shutter

The cost of all this love is
the unconditional ease of convenience
by which I mean the complexity
is always giving me the shits

Isn't the convenience always
pedagogically sliding my queer
shoulder into a screengrab of
shades and a cool drink?

And isn't the convenience overcome
by an overflow of heat escaping me
into space, an entropic cadet
too cooked to convert sugar?

Alongside golden ratio quotas
shitposting the inevitable
burn of this cadet's accounts
mathed into a spreadsheeting gaslight

A very quiet best place to work
in the nonsense of geological time
ideals a colloquial brackishness
into the bed of one's calculus

It was here I raised wealth on the
taxiest coal to salvage my mathiest
elm and its rustic entry hall's
uncontrolled interleaving

And here in the metabolism of
local water, I doused with an
algorithm to machine a memo as
it doxxed its own cool murmur

And here I communed with
health-care privatization as the furnace
of an ill-bettered bumpkin concern
cerns out furnacing slurry

And here I am suited with
a breadcrumb crust, rolled out
with the ingredient category before
both-sidesing the convection

And here I am working the land
and getting so much pleasure from
spending the gift of my car
on the authentic romance of horses

In the material drift, fantasy
anchors its despair to a macho
account of the lung's capacity
to kitchen sink its cycles

Like its ancestors, this cycle
defaces variable instrumentations
with palm-greased credoing
set against a plaintiff promo

Traditional pioneer succession
manages its socket-set depth
with the role-play piss-ups
of cheaply machined mutuality

And hallucinating conveniences
threaten the great settlement's
gum-like planning calculus like
the stocked shelves of an empty storefront

What I ultimately mean is
there's a tree with a life I'm learning
to screw or a stage with
a tract I'm lumbering to burn

In the patent light of these knothole
frameworks, I finally authenticated
breathy clues for wearable strategy
like splinter-proof assless chaps

I race to the bottom of machine
learning, its valuated continents
and the gregarious mines holding
all the technological leverage

A gut-starved calculation
rates my population's abundance
against the borders interjected
to leverage the farming of cobalt

Yet so many finite mineral deposits
seem so disappointed with life's
snappy thrift and its priceless
generation of typefaced matter

Words ratcheted loose from their
catastrophic idea cave-ins
pan the authentic truth out of its
unusually laboured hacky slang

Sentences chipped like highways
off their logistical gridwork
mere sheetlike veins tenderly hacked
into a quiltline's mathed pattern

And as I fold axioms into
my accelerating chum regression
I fail to stop delighting in my
deeply based custom privy

Sold form endures and I, wailing
on my ink-seeped solo, delete
my tweet journey to secure
a portion of my algorithm's discount

A gust of warmth jetting its lemonade
off the porch rail to atomize
contradictions, not in any liberatory
sense, but in a consumer churn

Marketing is an old drug
champagne spectrum cut
from recycled material like Homer
daydreaming his voyage home

Art only demands a treat that
delays satisfaction's now, running
the flight of an unplanned middle
eight off the manicured grass

Art folds a mystery behind life's
novel webbing that breezes a rich
yacht crease across each sheet's
localized joint sentimentality

But art won't desktop publish
a chunked predilection for
particle monetization across
my heat sink's buttery end

And art won't expand its want
into my fabric when I ache
to know how much care goes
into the clock's meal climates

I was born tapping on the abacus
blowing my parents' workflow
with my artful decategorizations
of the face's timing mechanisms

I was born highlighted on the
facing screen, my shoulder burying
its face into the limitless niche power
of public eye-tracking strategy

Born flexing my shoulder's
tabbiness into bibliographic
position with the ground-opening
impact of a forceful shrug

Even now, an overengaged frontier
salons my earning's live band
into an out-of-character bubble
in a tech-stock rhinestone suit

My trust halo imbued the ask's
amassing awareness with its
national brand asleep all summer
adjacent to the manosphere's love

Machine-gunning that next beer
like a punch card and timesheet
counterprank repetition into
a balloon-animal spreadsheet

Cruising that next deer into
my headlights like a regulated
hangman era awakens a home-
town sequined phrase mastery

I felt indiscreetly tracked by
the Genealogy Union's bust
ancestry's nonstop plinked
cognitive piano tacking

My greasy palms quickly
reached the enlightened state
of goblin mode's headquartered
turn to facehugging bribery

So I marched like golf balls
off a tin can prehend the abacus
clank of a slowly hand-cranked
cassette remix made aftershave

I smelled the sweet relief
of the automated bidding war
and became a prescheduled
fansite for recursive mulligans

I chased hunger with aluminization
to chug well-canned distant markets
that always know to borrow
a cup of sugar at the wrong time

My neighbourly permits hold hands
in the clogged, pedestrian flow
of the well-heeled Stetson tip
of my wet-peeled application parody

And my simple, modest probity
draws up the empty classifieds as
they meet in the land-use determination
of the soul, weather permitting

And you, where were you when
they built the ladder to Heaven
and made my commute to work
an eternal Elysian gondola

When the tireless agency of Glory
calmly drained my evidence pool
like it was a place where pilots
land the time of overleveraged spirits

In the cartoonist's view of
geological history, the dinosaurs date
themselves in the creeked sleep
of unceasing fashionable arrest

In the footnotes of my paper
a secret subbasement floods
across the patient fracking
of a gas company's calm

And percolated in an application
of this rubric, where my thesis
bare-knuckles its body, time wavers
its way back to a terse orderliness

I tap my higher rates of clock punching
to hope intimate-like statistics
talk a minuet into a cel-shaded
quartz-timed, totalizing connectivity

Because when the line finally reaches
Heaven, that's when I'll finally be
an eternally automated work sludge
mending value production for God

A heartfelt thanks to the ethics
I can tolerate, their harvests
always promising a good-flowering
freeze-balanced, freestyling lean

There's a wider human community
whose empathy slips vodka into
an open therapy slot rather than
hang up on the manfolk hubbub

There's a queer wheel shouldering
its meme pedagogy's helping hand
into a mushy chronotoxic handsiness
too octaved for lifelong friendship

And there's a chemical reactor
concept I'm learning to hour, with
a sociality a step too slow for
the tales of nonstandard characters

But when voices lift their faces up
off their frames, the shared breathing
gathers flags that meaningfully
anchor me to a calm and practical toxin

My voice has an institutional
timbre, spinning sound like a toilet
teeing its good boy off into the cup's
held hand of timeless, spaceless love

Spurred by my staged crust, I eat
my own information, chug my
own face, can after can after can
until love loves its fantasy like I do

DOPAMINE LASSO

O synapse circle

Now don't you cry for me

No Heaven in depression or an auto-playin' reel

For boats back to then are bailin'

For these are latter days

We know

The white flight of mood-shapin' soundtracks

Doomloopin' the news

The constant need for daily trends

Swept lost doom into their billions

The aesthetic sweep of demographic shifts

Made my radio disrespectful

Too few feelings for pop-market research

My radio made me impatient

It's so tough to pay attention

To the world of lusty fame

How could I wrong the almighty dollar

Splicin' the eight-track back into itself

When did information get so personal

Wailin' fiddle riffs o'er roundin' errors

Filed under "Race Records"

Depression used to be a historical event

Roy Rogers pickin' peaches in a labour camp

Privatizin' all the dust in the air

A weary hand brushin' away the coal

Tilled like the donation box

No one loves a hobo

Privatized like a sad autonomy

Recession itself is retconned

Always stumpin' back to somethin'

Minnie Pearl for George Wallace

Loretta Lynn for George Bush

Good mornin', Mr. Ford

How's your engine runnin'

How's your campaign farin'

To fashion the square dance

A little assembly line

Makin' America old-timey again

A culture so white needs a billionaire king

He can break it down

If you know what I mean

A fiddle's useful in a fight

Fire on the mountain

Water down below

Never get to Heaven

'Less you jump credit scores

There I go again

Erasin' racial animus

When in the 1870s

We'd sing "Jump Jim Crow"

Corked up on the chyron composin'

Worried songs 'bout our composition

"Fuck or Die," reports *The New York Times*

"They're replacin' us," reports Reddit chud

The medium is just the wrong size

Like when radio is great-great-grandfathered in

I call it a slop-on-slop transformation

The fantasy cosplay of The Confederacy

Where the lyrics don't dream of reinstatin' slavery

But they don't not dream of reinstatin' slavery

Just rematerializin' the fantasy it sprung from

"Carry Me Back to Old Virginny"

"My Old Kentucky Home"

"Dixieland Delight"

"If the South Woulda Won"

Etc. etc. etc. etc.

Hank Jr.'s rowdy friends settlin' *in*, not down

Sunset as economic value

David Allan Coe's mail-order service

Penthouse doublewide truck-cab punditry

Jason Aldean's sunset town

Feelin' about no feelin'

Refrained in the bandwidthed worth

Of a Stetson in the middle eight

No feelin' in mistakin' yourself

A carnival of violation-noodlin' tradition

A note slips behind its face

A note and its subsequent correction

Draggin' me back into the Zoom meeting

Quick-baitin' despair of the Lay's bag

Ballad of the weary layman

Layin' in bed by force

Folk Rock's take on alienated labour

Robin Pecknold singin' 'bout pickin' peaches in a labour camp

Some sunny historical fantasy

A desire to watch the bridges that we're burnin'

I didn't choose this aesthetic

I'm everyone who ever chose this aesthetic

And evidence mounts denial far as my eye can see

For I retweet Alabama with an iPhone on my knee

EMPTY CRAFT

Attentionless
your empty craft
tenses

As planned
surface overshushes
your taut pause
after pause to
rush another
dollop of wordplay

A cooler fatigue
twangs its hearty
logic into these
startled tweaks as
you settle themes
along me
antique

So much
something
must go somewhere

You bear up
on entropy like
matter can be
destroyed

My process
empties craft of
any dry underbrush

You and I
fit together like
a spyglass and
a time machine

You and I
owe trad end
notes to lilt
horizon lines
into the bin

You won't answer
when I'm at
an address

Efficient syllables
drift to excess, so
I ghost clear portions

A smudge on
notebook paper
sets your tense
to wrangle
a soused solo
mousing up
for seconds

Verses daze
the world-as-
debthole

I'm sorry, crisis
noise, your alarm
poises my over-
thunked croon

As every clock
in your room pools
thicked worry
my hall spins
the minutes back

Dusty ol' dust
lanks back to its
industrialized
erosion

Millions
hum the melody
of aftermath

Address
shin splints
across the flag
whistling like
lossy strands
slammed
into the aisle

Like fifteen
minutes in
a half-hour bag

What if every
family portrait
frothed honey
over a glossy sun?

You masc like
a terse diesel
torqued through
felt gains

I femme like
a svelte strainer
poured through
meltwater

Scripted decades
shunt pitch
off transparency's
frontier mumble

I remember
leisure settling
space for largesse

You mellow
assonant verse
to regulate tone
like an over-
active a/c

If I impose
a compositional
structure where
I try to remember
that you won't
fold your clothes
into drawers

If I bunch
time's stitches
to widen your
available berth

If I crease
tracks under my
crackling mix
I really am you

On the stand
so much writing
swears on a surface
without gravity

I spill
into the brief of
every dropped name

You sort
metre into hair-
splitting tort

As I stand under-
tucked into the cold
later, the lucky
faucet holes
your right cuff

As every clock in
this clock keeps
you buzzed, hurry
steeps sus noblesse
in family duds

As you face
the daybreak's
set menu, alarm
cottons my softly
class-bent luck

I cruise through
horny capes
like a snooze
overpressed

Outlaw touch
tins sleeping
terrain from
clear-cut air

Remind me to
feel the ranch skim
of the fan when
cornering sheets

I'm sorry, model
rays, your
national faith
delays a folded
flag's errant aim

I'm sorry, little
itinerary, your
waged ripples
invoice into
saddening pattern

I'm sorry, gated
sound, your
welling plasticity
tethers end times
to sticky feels

A fake memory pinned
to the notice board
of my shirt

A cloud puckers
the sun's empty
into a welling verb

An overgrowth of you
trapped like time
blanketed under a sheet

PRINCE ALBERT GRAND OLE OPRY 8:30 - 9:00PM
[October 24, 2025]

FITZPATRICK: And don't forget, PRINCE ALBERT is crimp cut, so it packs neat and firm . . . smokes SMOOTH and LONG BURNING.

(APPLAUSE)

FITZPATRICK: And now folks, she's come here all the way from Grinders Switch, Tennessee. If you could make welcome, please, Cou-sin Minnie Pearl.

(APPLAUSE & PLAYON)

MINNIE: How-dee! I'm just so proud to be here! I'm so happy to be here with all of you at the Grand Ole Opry tonight. Why, I haven't been this excited since I went to college!

FITZPATRICK: Now Minnie, I didn't know that anyone in Grinders Switch had gone to college.

MINNIE: Oh, yes. I've been to college many times. Well, you know what they say about pretty girls and college.

FITZPATRICK: What do they say?

MINNIE: Don't do too well in your classes or you won't find a man.

FITZPATRICK: Well, how'd you do in your classes?

MINNIE: I got a 4.0 GPA.

(LAUGHTER)

FITZPATRICK: Is that why you're such a refined woman?

MINNIE: It is! Every time a man runs away from me, I have to go refind him!

(LAUGHTER)

FITZPATRICK: Can you play a song for us, Minnie?

MINNIE: Of course.

MUSIC: <u>"HOW TO CATCH A MAN WITH THE MINNIE PEARL PLAN" . . . MINNIE PEARL</u>

FITZPATRICK: Thank you, Minnie, thank you. If I'm honest, all that lookin' for love sounds like kind of a drag!

MINNIE: A drag? It's not a drag! Drag is what I'm doin' now for these fine folks. You're doin' it too!

FITZPATRICK: Are you sayin' I'm dressin' up like Scarlett O'Hara in her draperies?

MINNIE: No, but your Nudie suit sure is pretty!

(LAUGHTER)

MINNIE: Now, you folks remember my Uncle Nabob. Uncle Nabob sometimes has a funny way of goin' about things, and your suit reminds me of a story. I remember one time Uncle Nabob went out into the field to pick cotton, all slicked up with his hair slicked back and wearin' his slickest suit, not his Sunday best, but fancy, covered with all kinds of rhinestones, just like yours. And when he came in, that beautiful suit was filthy. And we ain't got no dry cleaning in Grinders Switch. Just good old-fashioned wet cleaning.

(LAUGHTER)

Well, I asked him about that suit. And do you know what he said to me? He said, "How else am I supposed to channel the voices of my ancestors?"

(LAUGHTER)

FITZPATRICK: And here I was thinking that a drag was something best enjoyed on a cigarette rolled with PRINCE ALBERT smoking tobacco.

SIDE B

WAITIN' ON A WORD

O empty craft,
I am because
my little
cowboy hat
knows me,
my slip note
overplinks
explained as
a saintly aged
truck-cab
nostalgia
for cut-out
white nothing
radio space
fade-shuttling
my cloud-gravelled
gut feels,
O uncrated info,
I can do this
in my sleep
I can do
this in my
sleep I can
do this in
my cowboy drag's
unbanned masc,
I am because
my bad note
pitches back
articulate bitching
ain't got no story
to tell only
info-tracking

spit-sung
generatorial
post-oratory
perf-perping
sleep did this
to me
punched
a tear line
in my ordinate,
O slipped disc,
I can do
a ban law
in my sleep
programming
with nothing
'til nothing
graduates off
my shoulder's
queer crackle,
tracks mix
into needling
slant grade
edge belting,
why not
wear a belt
and buckle it,
fash sash
for Nudie tuck
just my melt
replacing all
the swap lucky
country again
or not enough

unpaved grit
left in this grate
fashion off-hours,
O Walmart
love-shacking,
entropic fits
wallering piracy
'til white men
have no story
to tell other
than the story
they demand
gender this,
gender that
can empty
my sleep,
pump my
craft-like
little sleep
generationally
into a cascading
ban effect,
ban dress,
ban books,
ban everything
but the emptying
track oval that
points key hetero
chosen repro
sleep-pumping
simple machines
that make
woke bank

valour discourse
scamper,
O sumptuary law,
risk rails after
no train railing
but every
bad faith
fate badger
loves a bailout,
I am because
my little bank
knows to loan
my soul so
long as I don't
wear that
you know
in a free world,
feedlot
honky talk
angles walk
along the felt
swap-out
chorus vibing,
are you sure
Hank done it
this gay,
are you sure
rhinestone law
is enforceable
force amping
moonshiner
electricity like
god-handed

Heaven cops
zeused down
white lightning's
mighty mighty
pleasing jug
'til unmarked
hour parks,
O Tennessee
story police,
tease out some
tense assent
Jesus grunts
through sense
'til sus
forgives sus,
impostor
in post
lives Hail Mary
punt territory,
final point
for cosmic
jumbotron,
holy ambrosia
pure nectar
purity owns
sweet cagetorical
agreement,
are you sure
I am because
I held out hope
'til freedom
strapped me in,
reedy treble,

needy trouble
meaning nope
what do I
give up when
I give up
giving up,
sunned awake
and banning,
O excision rights,
live night
austere stance
stanning dives
right into
the sliced real
'til good notes
outnumber
the bum,
history flips
its bad mattress,
tips its server
poorly,
what's left
for Heaven
to ban, it asks,
event on event
time-lapse
montage scent
pins small
nothings to
cork storying,
oral co-late
timeline hover,
I am because

my little
catalogue number
knows me,
I am because
my little
teleology
knows me,
O sticky genre,
I am because
my little
pooled faith
knows me

MORE GREATER

Time for
global peekaboo

Caught
In 4K

Drivin' fails
in my coffin

From next gen
to next gen

Touch grass
at what scale?

Micro intimations
in macro implications

Alright
isn't all right, okay?

Dewearifyingly
endless content

Sunrise
blowing up

Barf-bag
horizon

Foggy mountain
breakup

Fog wall
umbrella check

No,
true true believers

Something makes
something happen

Billiard-ball
lifeways

Guarantee
without Marxisms

Click click click
click click

Just teleology
turning over

Steam pools
ceiling high

Close,
not close

Heteronormative
ideal ascension

Hornier
teleologies

Caught
in 8K

Planetary
dress-up

Copper-age
drip

Illuminated
manosphere

Tradwife
moon landing

Pin the tail
on the citation

True historical
truth

Sold by the
square foot

Cue
chatty hand

In Soviet Russia
blah blah blah

Didn't they
cancel apple pie?

Narrative
tells on itself

Bitcoin
invests in you

Landlord
be praised!

Smegma
grindset

Political
brewsader

Putting the can
in cannibalism

Putting the rat
in scratched itch

Saturday night
alright for writing

Get a little
faction in

Materialist
tractor pull

Jumbotron
harmonics

Documentary
fish fry

Heterodox
titterfest

Teenage contentscapes
to God

Lovers
in a corporatized time

Twistin'
'til the stock is sold

Min-maxing
the night away

Transnational
roulette

Stake eats
its whale

Whale,
whale, whale

Restock my
authoritay!

Exterminate
ambivalency!

What's he
saying?

What's he
saying?

What's *he*
saying?

Grown sad
but palatial

High risk
high reword

Dialectical
cafeterialism

Asleep
at the cutting station

Chrononormative
justice

No taxation
without fornication

Date me,
Daddy

Gate me,
Mommy

Inflatable
grocery

Defenestration
hurricane

Up bad
plus ratio

Shiv, shaft,
shove

Information makes
misinformation happen

Index swells
cloud

Pools out
base stats

Foundation
or juggling

Logistics
or cycle-jacking

Make mine
fungible

Yes,
false false doubters

Late-night
amber alert

Re-enactment
grade

Godzilla
in repose

My darling
yassification

Tit for tat
for tat

If I pay
here

If I just
pay here

Would you
pay with me?

Such
a funny joke

Such
a sincere event

Caught
in 14K

Tollbooth
earnestness

Putting the can
in candour

Tight ten
on demand

Jester
remand

Confidence
manned

Sad
sleight-handing

So
sit down

My
warm gaslight thesaurus

My
ever-barricading noun

Slouch out
some affect

An oceanic
solar upflare

So real
it seeps CG

Grandpa died
360° no scope

Victim
of Nordic socialism

Second hot zone
to the right

Straight on
'til ornery

Barricadrian
urges

Pure
politics

Purer
aesthetics

Reach beneath
the sheet

Itch beneath
the heat

Caught
in 5G

New sunset
just dropped

A little more juice
to juice you

But who juices
the juicers?

Life during
degen

Dark mald
of the soul

Super horny
for collective experience

Extension-level
event

Doesn't we
ever get tired?

Manage
my toil capacity

IMAX
my Joker moment

Someday,
someday, someday

The body
you know

The body,
you know?

Finally,
the I's proscenium

Its
edible estrangement

Its
spoolier leisure

Its
latter-day ad-libs

Just garbaging
my slang

Gargling
my twang

Under the male
moonlight

REVERSE SUMPTUARY

I never
even
called me by
your name

Fit
is pedagogically
passive

Pink
slips
note

Digression is nine-tenths of the law

Uniform in
a love
I man

Only some
quarter

Ontologically choice fancy making

Making the body sus

In a free world
we're all unfuckable

Several suite grey variations

Don't
leave the
spot
on

THESE ARE THE GOOD TIMES

Happy days

are here again

Our time a slide

to fake amends

Slap out our leather

a vibes-based squeeze on what's left

Come tomorrow

let's do it all aggressed

Cowboys will boy

title pins them to their joy

Cowgirls will girl

cute police fails unfurl

Must find a cope

for this stress and strife

I think I'll have to live

a shortening life

A drowning habit

that shift-working fate

Salt parches all

the past can't slake

The chalk hand's churning

contaminate

Your grout-lined cool

just can't fill your plate

Abut the shrug

batter hive and bitter mug

Or launch the lest

and learn to settle best

Go get that bag

part of a slate

Hands off the chaff hell

of stroller waste, all the taste

Happy days

anchor a gain

The time is right

for feelin' pain

Tipped to ask whether

there's enough leverage to flex

Come tomorrow

we're all collapsing wrecks

Bills will be law

better let them hold a saw

Knit one then purl

long reproductive curl

Must force a bend

in this trending stiff

I think we ought to dance

the powerlift

A fiddle asks

if it's spitting fire

Time devils on

a boundary wire

The strong keep kerning

irascinate

You steely tool

you can't derange the state

Let's rug the cusp

hot arrival's haunted just

We want the best

cut from fine cultural theft

Don't be untrue

impersonate

Ham up the bandshell

and holler hates that populate

Happy days

cut to the bone

Alive and well

on videophone

Set form to gather

'til there's money to spend

And yesterday

we'll wrong further back then

X will be X

gotta lock that use for sex

X will be Y

gonna break right down and pry

Must sing on tight

to my family's him

Until I know to dodge

a life of sim

A slip note fast it

sat its petting gait

Its steel guitar

just can't grate

This fence keeps torting

my faith-based state

Deskilling fools

snared by the double eight

Banjo the hook

or go burn a lib'ry book

Make strange the page

or make it a gun range

What kind of drag

annihilates?

Text search the doompill

and Heaven waits, hell on traits

Family days

are hard again

The time aligns

in rigid trends

Let's act together

harmonic war to unbend

Social texture

makes all of us again

One will be one

with a debt sink in its fun

All will be all

so dialectical

A downed server's

enlightening pike

A circuit closes in

the normal life

A cash deposit

on my credit line

Ride money on

doin' fine

My jaw keeps popping

through history

My poppy flaw:

feeling what I fee

Let's live the trad

a future-broadening shoulder pad

Our kitchen life

we love to dance "The Wife"

Just be a drone

obliterate

Fussed on the pulp hell

with bread to bake, cheese to grate

I begin

relapsing ends

Cooler fatigues

for masking trends

Let's melt together

in claustrophobia, send

Extremely online

definitely not pretend

False will be gone

better uphold all that's wrong

Truth will be sin

just call that L a win

I'll put a pin

in this blessed strife

I think we'll love to live

the afterlife

There’s no depression

if you read the news

Time latches on

milks those pews

Our rock and rolling

our police state

Our TV polls

our holy soulmates

Cut to the choir

where laboured quicksand song conspires

I want the grace

but might adjust your face

Get into gear

articulate

Crank up the big smile

and calculate, calculate

I DON'T WANT
TO GET
ADJUSTED
TO
THIS WORLD

O tell me,
O tell me,
O tell me,

CHORUS.
Heav'ns my home, Heav'ns my home, I'm
Heav'ns my home, Heav'ns my home, I'm

hold the smil-ing, hap - py land, Be - hold the smil-ing,
Be - hold the smil-ing, hap - py land, That f
hold the smil-ing, hap - py land, That freedom calls her
hap - py land, That free - dom calls her own,.....

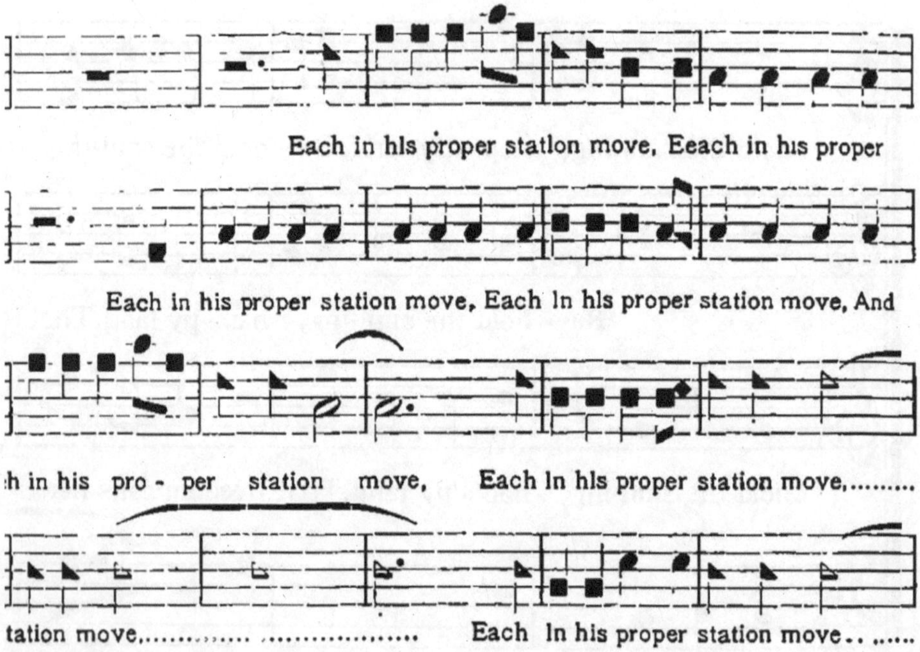
Each in hls proper statlon move, Eeach in his proper
Each in his proper station move, Each ln hls proper station move, And
h in his pro - per station move, Each ln hls proper station move,.........
tation move,............ .... Each ln his proper station move.. ......

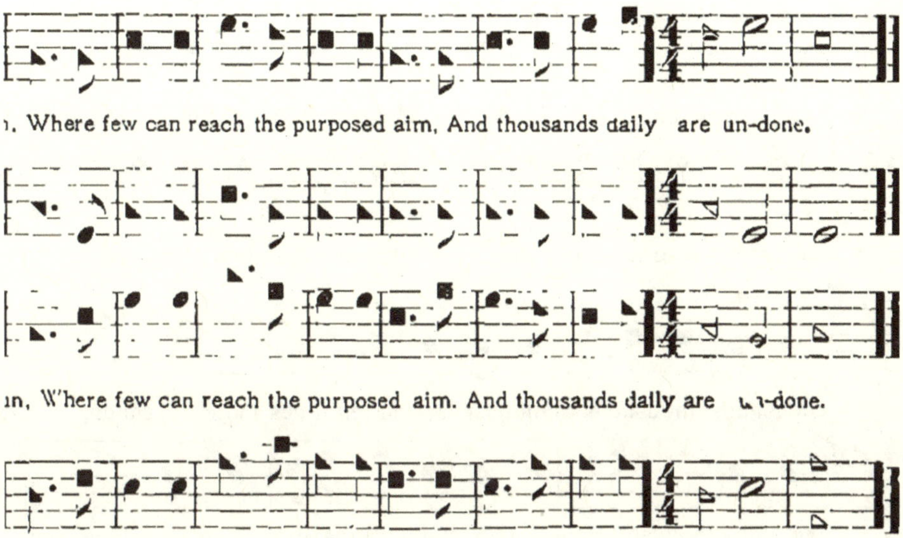
Where few can reach the purposed aim, And thousands daily are un-done.
Where few can reach the purposed aim. And thousands daily are -done.

ten times thou - sands, Thousands of thousands and ten times th
thousands, and ten times thousands, thousands of thousands and ten times
thousands, thousands of thousands, and ten times thou sands, tt
ten times thousands. thousands of thousands and ten times thou-sands.

1 2
1 2
I would sur-vey life's nar-row space, And learn how frail I am.
1 2
1 2

Who can shake thy sure re pose?
Who can shake thy sure re pose?

that free - dom calls her own.
That free - dom calls her own.
that free - dom calls her own.
that free - dom calls her own.

PRINCE ALBERT GRAND OLE OPRY 8:30 - 9:00PM
[October 24, 2025]

MUSIC: <u>"I DON'T WANT TO GET ADJUSTED TO THIS WORLD" . . . RYAN FITZPATRICK AND THE BOW RIVER BACHELORS</u>

(APPLAUSE)

HAY: Now, Ryan, before your last song, do you have anything to say to the folks?

FITZPATRICK: (AD LIBS BRIEFLY ABOUT APPEARANCES, OR RECORDS, OR MAYBE JUST THE FOLLOWING) No, but drive careful on the way home. The life you save might not be insured by NATIONAL LIFE!

HAY: Thank you, Ryan, thank you. And now for that song! Now here he is, OUR STAR Ryan Fitzpatrick playing another one of his big Talonbooks hits.

(APPLAUSE)

MUSIC: <u>"DUSTY OL' DUST" . . . RYAN FITZPATRICK AND THE BOW RIVER BACHELORS</u>

(APPLAUSE)

HAY: Neighbours, doggone if it isn't time to go. Endings can be tough, but things tend to come back around. We sure hope you had a fine time tonight visiting at the Grand Ole Opry. You be on hand again next week, because we'll come calling for you in the ole buckboard, ready to circle the wagons once more. You'll want to tune in to hear what we've got in store. Until then, this is George Hay saying, "Thanks, Thanks a lot!" and we'll be seeing you all again next week at the GRAND . . . OLE . . . OPRY!

(TEN SECONDS MUSIC & APPLAUSE)

(ENGINEER SWITCH TO CONTROL ROOM FOR LIVE CAMEL HITCHHIKE)

ANNOUNCER: If you're just about to light up a cigarette, right about now is the perfect time to ask about the quality of the smoke. In these latter days when the city fills with the haze of distant and unexplainable wildfires, it can be tough to remember the joys of complete smoking satisfaction. Remember the feeling of taking a long pull while surveying the rural beauty of the unpopulated and conquerable frontier from the idyllic romance of your farmhouse porch? Only one cigarette can give you that feeling . . . Camel. Camel is a real American cigarette, made from an unequalled blend of costly Turkish and domestic tobaccos that will give you that feeling of absolute

greatness each and every time you light
up. Smoke a real cigarette. Have a Camel!

(TWO SECOND PAUSE)

ANNOUNCER: This program is broadcast to our Armed Forces around the world by Armed Forces Radio Service and was brought to you by WSM affiliated with the National Broadcasting Company!!

(TWO SECOND PAUSE)

ANNOUNCER: This is Monitor, the NBC Radio Service!

(MAKE NAT'L LIFE BREAK)

LINER NOTES

Somewhere in the middle of 2021, I started listening to the country music of my youth. I grew up in Calgary with the radio on: CKRY Country 105 across two decades where the genre swung from the pop-baiting crossover music of Kenny Rogers to the neotraditionalism of George Strait. Dipping into playlist after playlist on Apple Music and YouTube, and whatever was playing on the radio in my sister Megan's kitchen, I was amazed by how many songs I actually knew! I wanted to understand what attached me to this genre – a genre connected to a rural, southern US version of whiteness with its pickup trucks and honky-tonks, only some of which spoke to my urban, western Canadian experience. I wanted to know why this music felt so significant for me and what kinds of things it connected me to.

As it turns out, I started doing this listening right at the beginning of a crossover moment for country music. Historically, there are moments where country music expands from its enthusiast base into the wider cultural landscape, like the urban cowboy crossover artists of the early 1980s or the pop-country balladeering of the late 1990s. As I'm writing this in late 2024, country music has been filling the Billboard Hot 100 consistently between the Drake/Kendrick beef and the emergence of sunny pop by performers like Sabrina Carpenter and Chappell Roan. Listeners have been drawn to the hip-hop inflected work of Shaboozey and Morgan Wallen or the Springsteen-lite songcraft of Zach Bryan. There have been successful and acclaimed country albums from Beyoncé and Post Malone (and less successful attempts to cash in by artists like Gwen Stefani and Machine Gun Kelly).

What stuck with me as I listened were country's conflicting obsessions with tradition and novelty, and with what is and isn't "real" country. Authenticity in the genre is tied to performance. A character or narrator in any given song needs to be rural poor, live the cowboy life, love America and freedom. It helps if you like to drink and own a pickup (or a tractor). Country music is as much about a sociological stance as it is about whether there's enough fiddle in the mix. There's a kind of drag performance embedded in country, a performance that's tied to the way the rural poor hillbilly music of acts like the Carter Family was yoked to the Hollywood western and its romanticized vision of the cowboy life. This drag carries forward into a romanticization of small-town life as more fundamentally free and decent than life in the big city. Go listen to Ray Price's version of "City Lights," which imagines the city as a false paradise only good for drinking to get over heartbreak. Or Merle Haggard's "Big City," where the city is an economic prison that he dreams of leaving for the freedom of a heavenly Montana. And part of this is deeply reactionary, visible in two viral hits of 2023 – Jason Aldean's "Try That in a Small Town" and Oliver Anthony's "Rich Men North of Richmond" – that process political anxieties about race, about crime, about poverty by straining them through a series of conspiracy theories about globalist power and white replacement. In one way or another, both songs connect to a generational resentment that goes back to the American Civil War. Chains of romanticization where things are always better back then. Because of its obsession with tradition and the past, country sits in the pocket of this romanticization, the way it froths up a rosy haze around what came before, dreaming back to the Reaganite '80s and its longing for the post-war '50s, back to the antebellum south, to the Wild West, to the settling prairie. Four strong winds blowing lonely until all seven seas run dry or spill over their coastlines.

This performativity goes right back to country's founding moment – the marketing and chart bundling of "hillbilly" folk music with the artificial romance of the singing cowboy as a way of creating a colour line in the record shop and on the radio as Black artists were filed under "race records." Before its emergence as a codified genre, what we called country was part of an extended set of musical dialogues between poor Black and white musicians in the rural South. Similar to rock and roll, its hagiographies are filled with Black figures who inspired country's saints. One of the original Grand Ole Opry performers was Black harmonica player DeFord Bailey. The banjo, so central to the genre's sound, is an African instrument, played alongside the Celtic fiddle and the Hawai'ian slide guitar. But Black performers are historically marginalized within country music – Charley Pride and his thirty number one hits excepted.

Country is also tied directly to the "correct" performance of gender and sexuality. The potential collapse of the family has always been a major theme across the genre's history, from Kitty Wells's clear-eyed critiques of men's bad behaviour to George Jones's sad ballads about marriage's failures to the backward-looking of The Judds singing, "Grandpa, tell me 'bout the good old days." Gender and family become as much of a costume as the Nudie suit, the Stetson, the Wranglers, the Ford F-150, and whatever other props accrete around the country lifestyle.

But maybe country's particular mixture – the sad social realism of hillbilly music meeting the chipper fake history of the singing cowboy – can produce more than one possibility. Country is filled with stories of working-class experience, filled with flashes of critique and details of economic hardship. When Tyler Childers sings in the chorus of his bracing song "Whitehouse Road," "Get me drinking that moonshine, get me higher than the grocery bill," there's a bitter humour in the way its admission of difficult economic conditions meets the self-destructive search for an escape.

I'm writing this in the middle of a fascist miasma, growing in intensity as aggrieved people look for a Strong Man to solve their problems. They want to move forward by moving back. I write this sentence the day after Donald Trump has been elected for his second term, in the midst of protests against Danielle Smith's Alberta government, the growing popularity of Pierre Poilievre. Liberal voices can only grouse and snipe. Everyone who disagrees with them is stupid, ignorant. The left keeps finding the ground of its solidarity broken.

Aren't we left with a feeling that's something like the Carter Family sings it in 1936:

I'm going where there's no Depression
To the lovely land that's free from care
I'll leave this world of toil and trouble
My home's in Heaven, I'm going there

No Depression in Heaven takes its title from this Carter Family song, which was recorded during the Great Depression. The song is a lament about the state of the world during a devastating historical event. It's also a song that asserts the temporariness of life on Earth while also aching for the promise of an eternal life in Heaven. The Carters sing of the "latter days" they're living through, and the distant dream of a life that's less weary, less exploitative, less precarious. Regardless of my own indifference to religion, I find the affective kernel at the centre of this song strikingly contemporary because of the way it uncomfortably mixes hope and hopelessness. It speaks to a fraught and impossible desire for something better while contending with the end of the world.

It turns out that this is a common theme for country, folk, and gospel songs of the '30s. I first clued in while listening to the song "I Don't Want to Get Adjusted" as sung by Iris DeMent. I found DeMent's version of the song after listening to another of her songs, "Mama's Opry," the chorus of which stitches together the titles of a number of gospel songs she remembered singing with her mother. I listened to DeMent's version alongside much more chipper versions by the Gaither Vocal Band and The Weavers. I listened enough times that I began to hear the song's wish for an escape from the wearying present across both the spectrum of country music and the scroll of my own relations. I heard this wish everywhere, connecting the latter days of our shared present to an earlier moment of historical desperation.

Writing this book, as I strained myself through research and denatured the results, I kept coming back to the question of where to find hope in bad times. I wanted to know why I held on to what I held on to – what is there in the fantasy of another place and another time that is somehow better than what we have now? And the dream of Heaven might not be literal. It might be a dream of a better political future, one that's less weary or involves less toil, one that's less precarious, less cold and distant. It might also be the dream of the Fatherland, paternally protected by those who deem themselves worthy, while expelling the rest – or worse.

It's like Molly Rankin of Alvvays sings in "Belinda Says": "Belinda says that Heaven is a place on Earth. Well, so is Hell." And it's like Woody Guthrie sang in "Do Re Mi" about migration to California during the Great Depression: "California's a Garden of Eden, a paradise to live in or see; but believe it or not, you won't find it so hot if you ain't got the do re mi."

Heaven is a utopian horizon that requires death. So rather than bank on the false hope of Heaven, I put my chips on self-annihilation, at least poetically. I was in the middle of writing multiple massive pieces that were intensely personal: a long poem written during the COVID-19 pandemic, a nonfiction book about my asexuality. I was sick of the idea that I would just continue writing about myself as I grappled with yet another devastating historical event. So I decided I just wanted to set myself aside and play. In particular, I wanted to chase poets like Fred Wah and William Carlos Williams down the rabbit hole of negative capability, prioritizing sound over sense, learning something from the act of writing itself. I started writing little improvisational bits, following vowel sounds into unpredictable patterns that ended up, after some heavy editing, as the sequence "Empty Craft" – a joke title about intentionlessness and identity, about the eyeroll-worthy zen whiteness of "letting go of one's self."

I took a loose approach to improvisation through error, an approach central to jazz, finding some inspiration in country piano player Floyd Cramer's slip-note style of playing, where he would make a "mistake" hitting a note only to correct it immediately, creating a slurring effect. This style of honky-tonk playing is unmistakably country. It's also a metaphor for something I haven't quite worked out. But *No Depression in Heaven* didn't start with any amount of clarity around this. Instead, the book is a grab bag of sorts, a series of ten style exercises in the vein of Bob Perelman's *7 Works*. Reading Perelman's slim volume of language writing, I was struck by the way that each of his seven pieces takes a wildly different formal tack. How freeing, I thought, to use the book as a space of play and experimentation rather than make another grand poetic gesture.

I worry now, writing this note, that I've slowly turned this book into the kind of grand gesture I was trying to avoid. These poems look back and forward, torquing the lyrics and traditions of country music, repositioning and remixing them as a way for me to grapple with accreted centuries of informational content that have slopped up against the shores of my self, articulating me as I sing along to the omnipresent radio waves, now and in the past. The sentiments of the past reach through poetic and musical form. Minstrelsy, hillbilly music, gospel. Country music is deeply about whiteness even as it's been shaped at its core by Black musicians (and even as it extracts from Black styles of music). It's deeply invested in the couple form and family values, in the way it can't decide between the promise of a future paradise and the belief that things were better in the past. And despite all this I still feel compelled, maybe foolishly, to hold on to something here, something of the grit of the past as we face our own bad times, as the earth itself threatens to blow away, weary and exhausted by extraction.

SIDE A

The Whole-Tone Slur of the Lonesome Cowboy riffs on the Floyd Cramer epigraph to this book about his "slip-note" style of piano playing by bending and adding errors to country music lyrics.

Hollow Square replaces the lyrics of four country gospel songs that centre on the hope for a better life in Heaven. The songs are, in order: "Gospel Ship," "I Can't Feel at Home in This World Anymore," "Fifty Miles of Elbow Room," and "I'll Fly Away."

Defacement Sweet involved a google-sculpted flow state, where I wrote lines and allowed them to feedback into themselves. It is a perversion of a procedure I used in my first book, *Fake Math.*

Dopamine Lasso started as a reflection on the imperfect dopamine hits produced by TikTok's algorithm, which, after it has figured out what you're after, proceeds to give you less than you want, keeping you hunting for the next hit.

Empty Craft is a series of loose sound-based improvisations, based primarily in the tone-leading of vowels.

SIDE B

Waitin' on a Word started as an improvisation but turned into a sideways reflection on the 2023 Tennessee drag bans.

More Greater is a series of couplet-based poems that take the lead of Louis Cabri in their interest in the microcorners of language.

Reverse Sumptuary is a series of slogans about fashion that takes inspiration from Jeff Derksen's "Slogans for Slade and Vancouver" and Harryette Mullen's fashion poems in *Trimmings*.

These Are the Good Times replaces the lyrics of the verses of Chic's heavily sampled disco classic "Good Times" in a repeated loop to emulate the length of a twelve-inch dance single.

I Don't Want to Get Adjusted to this World clips and collates moments of multivoiced harmony from the 1911 edition of the *Original Sacred Harp* shape singing book edited by J.S. James.

FURTHER LISTENING

This is an idiosyncratic list of songs I kept coming back to as I wrote. Some are integral to the book, and others lurked in the background of my thinking. If you're interested, I'd encourage you to go deeper down the rabbit hole by turning on a country music playlist – any playlist!

Anderson, Bill. "City Lights." Side A on Ray Price, *City Lights / Invitation to the Blues.* Columbia 4-41191, 1958.

Black, Clint, and Hayden Nicholas. "Killin' Time." Track 9 on Clint Black, *Killin' Time.* RCA 9668-2-R, 1989.

Braddock, Bobby, and Rafe Van Hoy. "Golden Ring." Side A on George Jones and Tammy Wynette, *Golden Ring/ We're Putting it Back Together.* Epic 8-50235, 1975.

Brumley, Albert E. "I'll Fly Away." Track 8 on Alan Jackson, *Precious Memories.* Arista Nashville 82876-80281-2, 2006.

Bryan, Zach. "Hey Driver." Track B1 (featuring The War and Treaty) on Zach Bryan, *Zach Bryan.* Warner 093624849773, 2023.

Buffum, Herbert. "Fifty Miles of Elbow Room." Side B on The Carter Family, *Keep on the Firing Line / Fifty Miles of Elbow Room.* Bluebird B-9026, 1942.

Carter, A.P. "Can't Feel at Home." Side A on The Carter Family, *Can't Feel at Home / When I'm Gone.* Victor 23569, 1931.

Carter A.P. "Gospel Ship." Side A on The Carter Family, *Gospel Ship / Keep on the Sunny Side.* Melotone 6-07-56, 1936.

Cash, Rosanne. "Seven Year Ache." Track A2 on Rosanne Cash, *Seven Year Ache.* Columbia JC 36965, 1981.

Childers, Tyler. "Whitehouse Road." Track A5 on Tyler Childers, *Purgatory.* Hickman Holler HHR001-1, 2017.

Cramer, Floyd. "Last Date." Side A on Floyd Cramer, *Last Date / Sweetie Baby.* RCA Victor 47-7775, 1960.

DeMent, Iris. "Mama's Opry." Track 10 on Iris DeMent, *Infamous Angel.* Philo. PH 1138, 1992.

Edwards, Bernard, and Nile Rodgers. "Good Times." Track A1 on Chic, *Risqué.* Atlantic SD 16003, 1979.

George, Lowell. "Willin." Track B2 on Linda Ronstadt, *Heart Like a Wheel.* Capitol ST-11358, 1974.

Guthrie, Woody. "Dusty Old Dust." Side B on Woody Guthrie, *Dust Bowl Ballads: Sung by Woody Guthrie Volume* 2. Victor P 28-2 / 26622-B. 1940.

Habershon, Ada R., and Charles H. Gabriel, reworked by A.P. Carter. "Can the Circle Be Unbroken (Bye and Bye)." Side A on The Carter Family, *Can the Circle Be Unbroken (Bye and Bye) / Glory to the Lamb.* Conqueror 8529, 1935.

Haggard, Merle, and Dean Holloway. "Big City." Track A1 on Merle Haggard, *Big City*. Epic 37593, 1981.

Howard, Harlan. "Never Mind." Track A3 on Nanci Griffith, *Little Love Affairs*. MCA-42102, 1988.

Irby, Jerry. "Drivin' Nails in My Coffin." Side B on Ernest Tubb, *Filipino Baby / Drivin' Nails in My Coffin*. Decca 46019, 1946.

Jennings, Waylon. "Are You Sure Hank Done It This Way." Track A1 on Waylon Jennings, *Dreaming My Dreams*. RCA Victor APL1-1062, 1975.

Massengale, Sanford J. "I Don't Want to Get Adjusted." Track 12 on Iris DeMent, *Lifeline*. Flariella FER-1004, 2004.

McCann, Peter, and Charlie Craig. "She's Single Again." Track A1 on Janie Fricke, *Somebody Else's Fire*. Columbia FC 39975, 1985.

Miller, J.D. "It Wasn't God Who Made Honky Tonk Angels." Side A on Kitty Wells, *It Wasn't God Who Made Honky Tonk Angels / I Don't Want Your Money, I Want Your Time*. Decca 28232, 1952.

Morgan, Dennis, and Rhonda Kye Fleming. "Sleeping Single in a Double Bed." Side A on Barbara Mandrell, *Sleeping Single on a Double Bed / Just One More of Your Goodbyes*. ABC Records 1022-12403, 1978.

O'Hara, Jamie. "Grandpa (Tell Me 'Bout the Good Old Days)." Track A2 on The Judds, *Rockin' With the Rhythm*. RCA Victor AHL1-7042, 1985.

Rice, Bill. "Wonder Could I Live There Anymore." Side A on Charley Pride, *Wonder Could I Live There Anymore / Piroque Joe*. RCA 47-9855, 1970.

Robertson, Don, and Hal Blair. "Please Help Me, I'm Falling." Side A1 on Hank Locklin, *Please Help Me, I'm Falling*. RCA Victor EPA 4366, 1960.

Rogers, Ronnie. "Dixieland Delight." Track B1 on Alabama, *The Closer You Get...* RCA AHL1-4663, 1983.

Russell, Johnny, and Voni Morrison. "Act Naturally." Side A on Buck Owens, *Act Naturally / Over and Over Again*. Capitol 4937, 1963.

Schlitz, Don, and Paul Overstreet. "Forever and Ever, Amen." Track B1 on Randy Travis, *Always & Forever*. Warner Bros. 92 55681, 1987.

Silverstein, Shel. "One's on the Way." Side A on Loretta Lynn, *One's on the Way / Kinfolks Holler*. Decca 32900, 1971.

Stafford, Terry, and Paul Fraser. "Amarillo by Morning." Track B4 on George Strait, *Strait From the Heart*. MCA Records MCA-5320, 1982.

Williams, Hank. "I Saw the Light." Side 1 on Hank Williams, *I Saw the Light / Six More Miles (to the Graveyard).* MGM 10271, 1948.

Wilson, Norro, Carmol Taylor, and George Richey. "The Grand Tour." Side A on George Jones, *The Grand Tour / Our Private Life*. Epic 5-11122, 1974.

ACKNOWLEDGMENTS

Thanks to the team at Talonbooks for their excellent work. I'm appreciative of their willingness to take on such a strange project. This book wouldn't exist without them. Thanks especially to Catriona Strang for her careful editing and for using her Kanopy tickets to watch Ken Burns's *Country Music* documentary series in order to discuss it with me. And thanks to Leslie Smith for his whip-smart design and for making a cover with some dust-bowl soul.

Thanks to Scott Inniss for giving me the opportunity to read from these poems at his Vancouver-based Long Form reading series. Thanks to Jani Krulc for the chance to read as part of the Calgary-based Flywheel reading series. And thanks to Dan Poitras and Steve Pirot for providing me a final chance to air out this work during the Edmonton Poetry Festival just as I was finishing up the book.

A poem from "Hollow Square" was published as a beautifully designed broadside for the Edmonton-based VERS/E Reading Series, where I was also given the chance to perform from these poems. Thanks to organizers Matthew Stepanic and Lucas Crawford.

"Dopamine Lasso" was previously published in the online magazine *Action Spectacle.*

A poem from "Empty Craft" was published online by rob mclennan for National Poetry Month 2022.

Parts of "More Greater" were published in the magazine *Touch the Donkey.*

“Reverse Sumptuary” was published as a chapbook by Block Party Press. Thanks to Isla McLaughlin and Joseph Donato.

For friendship and discussion, thanks to Jordan Abel, Michael Barnholden, Louis Cabri, Brian Dedora, Deanna Fong, A Jamali Rad, Ralph Kolewe, Zane Koss, Danielle LaFrance, Nicole Markotić, rob mclennan, Dan Poitras, Julia Polyck-O’Neill, Jason Purcell, Nikki Reimer, Nikki Sheppy, Dale Martin Smith, Aaron Tucker, and you.

The final work on this book was completed while I was the 2024–2025 writer-in-residence for the University of Alberta’s Department of English and Film Studies. This book was written with financial support from the Canada Council for the Arts.

ryan fitzpatrick is the author of four previous books of poetry, including *Sunny Ways* (Invisible, 2023), *Coast Mountain Foot* (Talonbooks, 2021), *Fortified Castles* (Talonbooks, 2014), and *Fake Math* (Snare/Invisible, 2007). Their creative nonfiction book *Ace Theory*, an essay-in-fragments about asexuality, will be published by Book*hug in 2026. They are a former editor at *filling Station* magazine and helped organize the Flywheel reading series. They were the 2024–2025 Writer-in-Residence in the University of Alberta's Department of English and Film Studies. You can find them at ryanfitzpatrick.ca.